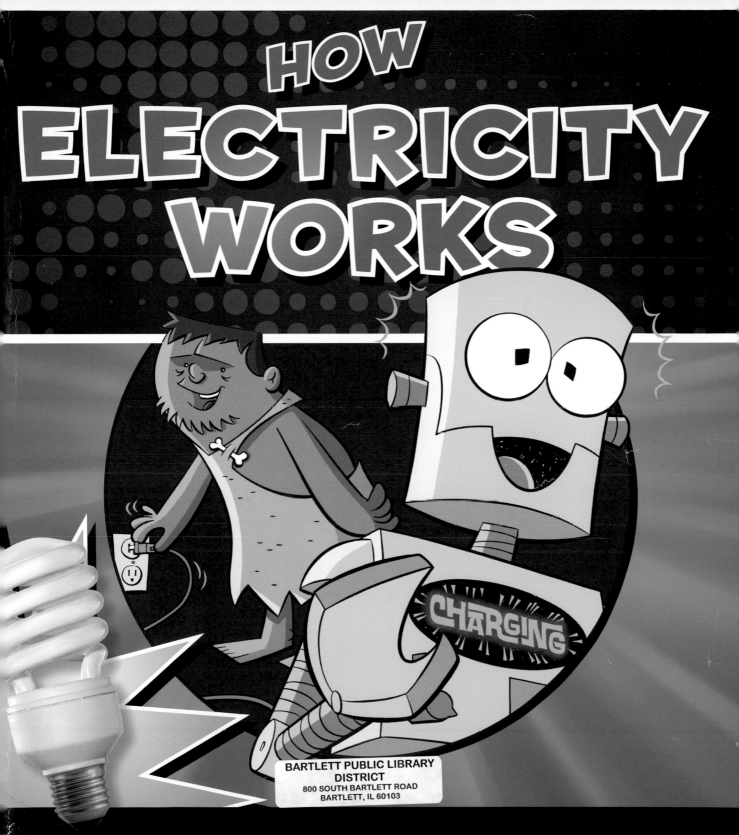

HOW ELECTRICITY WORKS

BY JENNIFER SWANSON • ILLUSTRATED BY GLEN MULLALY

Published by The Child's World®
1980 Lookout Drive • Mankato, MN 56003-1705
800-599-READ • www.childsworld.com

ACKNOWLEDGMENTS
The Child's World®: Mary Berendes, Publishing Director
Content Consultant: Paul Ohmann, PhD, Associate
  Professor of Physics, University of St. Thomas
The Design Lab: Design and production
Red Line Editorial: Editorial direction

LIBRARY OF CONGRESS
CATALOGING-IN-PUBLICATION DATA
Swanson, Jennifer.
  How electricity works / by Jennifer Swanson ;
illustrated by Glen Mullaly.
      p. cm.
  Includes bibliographical references and index.
  ISBN 978-1-60973-216-5 (library reinforced : alk. paper)
  1. Electricity—Juvenile literature. I. Mullaly, Glen, 1968- ill.
II. Title.
  QC527.2.S93 2012
  537--dc22   2011010916

Photo Credits © Murat Giray Kaya/iStockphoto, cover,
1; T.A.E. Inc./Library of Congress, 5; Konstantin Kirillov/
iStockphoto, 6; H. S. Sadd/Library of Congress, 8, 22;
Baris Simsek/iStockphoto, 9; Fotolia, 12; Nikita Sobolkov/
iStockphoto, 17; Eliza Snow/iStockphoto, 18; iStockphoto,
23 (top), 24 (middle), 24 (top right); Paula Connelly/
iStockphoto, 24 (top left); Jacques Arpin/iStockphoto,
25 (top); Kyle Nelson/iStockphoto, 25 (bottom); Library of
Congress, 23 (bottom); Spectral-Design/iStockphoto, 24
(bottom right); Alfred T. Palmer/Library of Congress, 24
(bottom left)

Printed in the United States of America in Mankato,
Minnesota.
July 2011
PA02092

ABOUT THE AUTHOR
Jennifer Swanson's first love is science,
and she is thrilled to be able to combine
that with her passion for writing. She has
a bachelor of science in chemistry from
the US Naval Academy and a master of
science in education science from Walden
University. Jennifer is currently employed
as a middle school science instructor for
Johns Hopkins University's Center for
Talented Youth.

ABOUT THE ILLUSTRATOR
Glen Mullaly draws neato pictures for kids
of all ages from his swanky studio on the
west coast of Canada. He lives with his
awesomely understanding wife and their
spectacularly indifferent cat. Glen loves
old books, magazines, and cartoons, and
someday wants to illustrate a book on How
Monsters Work!

TABLE OF CONTENTS

CHAPTER ONE

POWER UP!

You walk into your house at night. What is the first thing you do? Turn on the light, of course. Next you turn on the television, check your messages, and maybe even get a snack out of the fridge. What makes all this possible? Electricity!

Do you ever stop to think what your life would be like without electricity? Most people don't, unless there's a power outage. But hundreds of years of trial and error and hard work went into powering those appliances you turn on with the flip of a switch.

Imagine you lived 60, 125, 150, or even 2,000 or more years ago. How would your world be different?

60 YEARS AGO Electricity was widespread in US cities. Nearly all farms and rural homes had recently been wired as well.

125 YEARS AGO By now, Thomas Edison's light bulb had been around for just a few years. It could stay lit for up to 150 hours. In 1882, Edison had also opened the first power station, in New York City. It was capable of powering 5,000 lights. The age of electricity was born.

Edison at work in his laboratory

The electric motor had been invented in 1837, but it still wasn't clear how this could help bring electricity to houses. People used gas lanterns in their homes at night. The gas could be dangerous. If it built up in an enclosed room, it made people sick or worse.

People were aware of a great energy in lightning storms, but most were afraid of lightning. The ancient Greeks had discovered static electricity around 600 BC. People lit their homes with fire and torches.

Electric wires start the engines in our cars. They charge the batteries that run our MP3 players, cell phones, and ATMs. Engineers are developing electric cars to help reduce pollution. It's hard to imagine a world without electricity!

DANGEROUS KITE

An artist's sketch of Franklin's famous electricity experiment

Ben Franklin was the first person to discover that lightning was caused by electricity. In 1752, he described his famous experiment. First, he attached a pointed wire to a homemade kite. At the end of the kite's string, he fastened a metal key. Then, he flew the kite during a thunderstorm. Zap! Lightning struck the kite, giving him a large shock. That proved that electricity had traveled from the metal wire, down the string, and to the key in his hand.

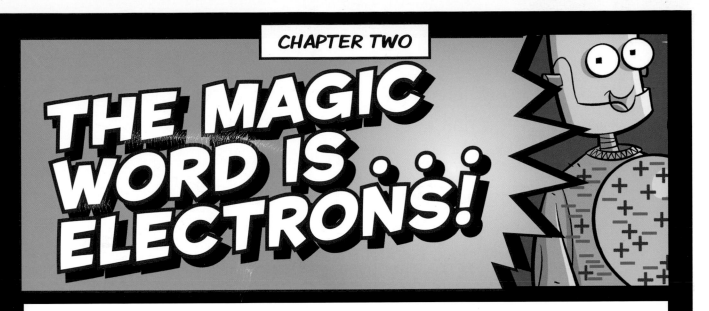

CHAPTER TWO

THE MAGIC WORD IS ... ELECTRONS!

Electricity is a form of energy older than Earth itself. And it begins in the smallest unit of matter—the atom. Atoms are so small, they can be seen only with the most powerful microscopes. But atoms make up everything in the world: clouds, cars, computers—even you!

Inside an atom are even tinier particles called protons and **electrons**. Protons are found in the center of the atom. Electrons spin tightly around this center.

Atoms combine in structures like this to make up everything around us.

Protons and electrons are opposite in one important way. A proton has a positive charge. That charge is marked by a plus sign (+). An electron has a negative charge. Scientists show that with a minus sign (–). A proton's charge is exactly opposite of an electron's charge. So, the two cancel each other out perfectly.

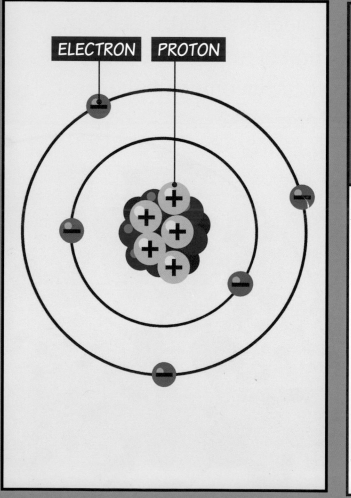

ELECTRON   PROTON

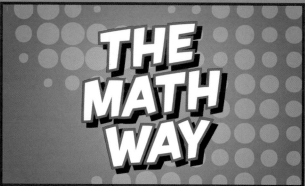

Do you like math? Then, think of charge this way:
1 proton equals +1.
1 electron equals −1.
So, 1 proton + 1 electron = 0
or

$$\begin{array}{r} +1 \\ + \ -1 \\ \hline 0 \end{array}$$

Electrons on the Loose

Zero charge is the goal when it comes to atoms. That's why opposites attract. Protons and electrons pull on each other so everything stays nice and balanced. Still, sometimes electrons get excited. They break free from an atom and zip around by themselves. This flow of electrons is what creates electricity.

Think of it this way. Take a balloon and hold it against your shirt. Does it stay? Nope. Now rub the balloon back and forth against your shirt about ten times. Then let go of it. Does it stick to your shirt? Yep. What changed?

Electrons did. Some of the electrons in the balloon were knocked off by the rubbing. They jumped to your shirt—it took on a negative charge. Meanwhile, the balloon was left with more protons than electrons. It took on a positive charge. Since opposites attract, your shirt was attracted to the balloon. Electricity made them stick together.

STATIC ELECTRICITY

There are two kinds of electricity. An electric current runs through the wires in your house. This kind of electricity powers your world.

The other kind is static electricity, and it happens by accident all the time. Static electricity might make your clothes stick together in the dryer and crackle when you pull them apart. Or it gives you a surprise shock when you touch the metal handle on your desk drawer. Static electricity comes from friction, or things rubbing against each other.

Did you know lightning is a form of static electricity? As rain clouds move around in the sky, they rub against each other. Electrons break away. Together, they create a huge electric charge.

Soon, the electric charge gets too great. It must be balanced out. Zap! Flash! The electrons "ride" a bolt of lightning to a positive charge, either in another cloud or on the ground.

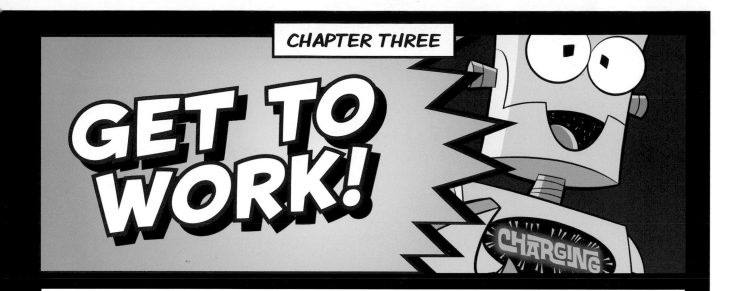

CHAPTER THREE

GET TO WORK!

So how do we make electricity work for us? First, we have to make sure the electrons flow the way we want them to. That sounds like a job for . . .

1. AN ELECTRIC CIRCUIT

An **electric circuit** is a closed loop that allows electrons to flow all the same way. Let's see how it works:

The electrons zip from the battery to the bottom of the light. The light turns on, but that is not the end of the story. The electrons keep going until they reach the other end of the battery. Here, they find a positive charge.

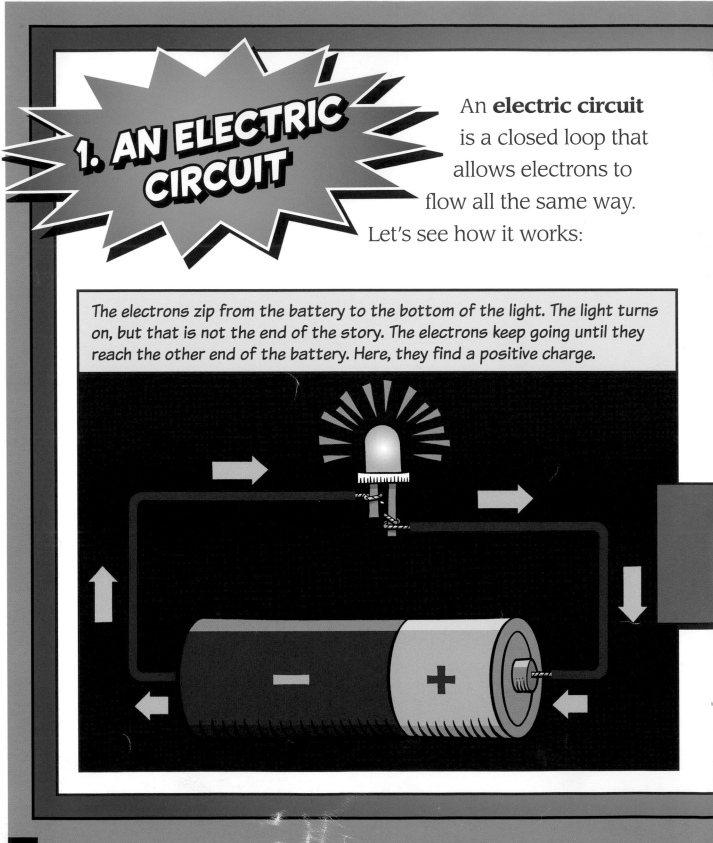

LIGHTS, PLEASE

How does a lamp turn on and off? When the switch is turned to OFF, the circuit is open. No electricity flows. Switching to ON closes the circuit. Electricity flows to the lamp, and it lights up.

A circuit works only if the path is complete. If there's a gap, the electrons can't find their way to the end. They get confused and stop moving. That means there isn't a current.

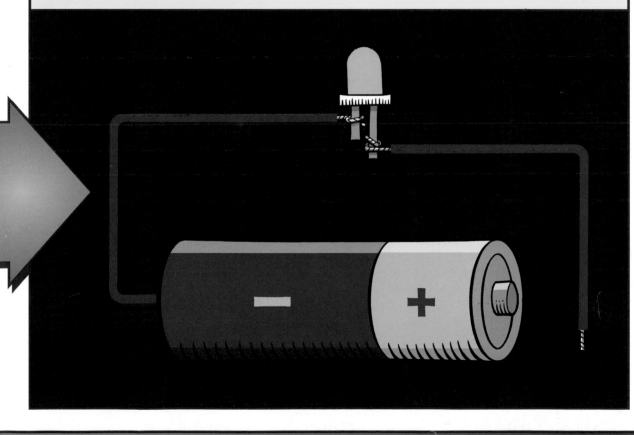

2. CONDUCTORS

I am an excellent conductor!

So, can you use any type of wire to create a circuit? No. A lot of substances don't allow electrons to flow through them. They include rubber, glass, plastic, and cloth. But **conductors** let electrons zip right through. Copper wire is an example of an excellent conductor.

Hmmm. And yet, those cords plugged in all around your house look like they're made of plastic or rubber. You can probably figure out why. The metal wires are inside the plastic coating—and lucky for you. The coating keeps you from getting a bad shock.

3. MAGNETS

Magnets create a force called *magnetism*, which is closely linked to electricity. Spinning magnets cause electrons to move in nearby wires. Power plants use this idea to make electricity.

CHAPTER FOUR

AT THE POWER PLANT

A single power plant can generate enough electricity to power thousands of homes. How does it work?

A power plant has a **generator**, which contains a large magnet surrounded by wires. Attached to the generator is a turbine—a series of big wheels. These are turned either by wind, steam, or water. When the turbine spins, so does the magnet inside the generator. This causes the electrons in the wires to move. Electricity is created!

Generators working at a dam

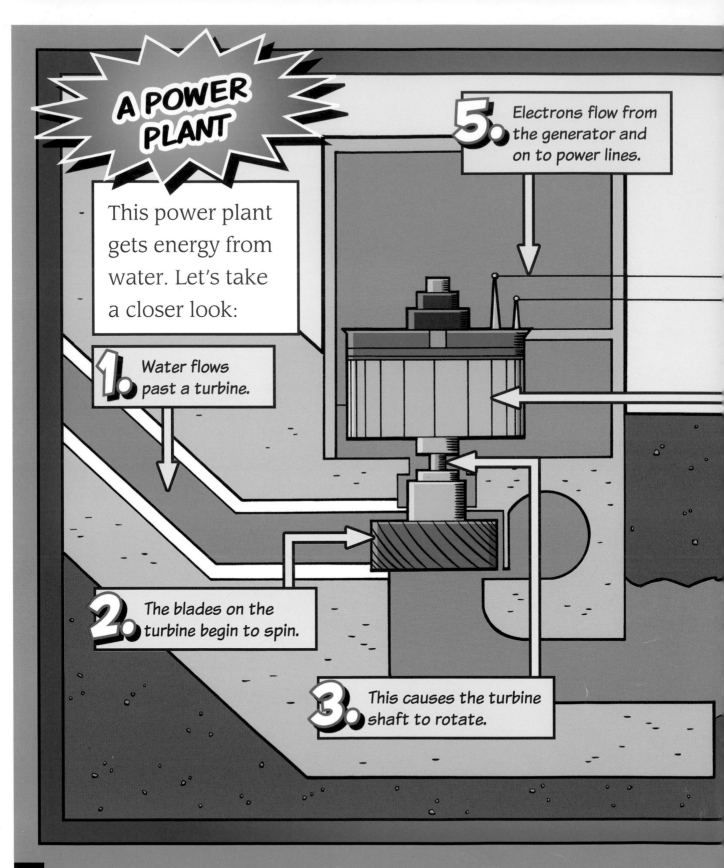

4. The magnets in the generator spin around the shaft.

POWER SOURCES

Power plants need energy to spin those turbines. They can get it from water, steam, or wind.

1. Water: The turbines are set below the water flow. Gravity pulls the water past the turbines, making them turn.

2. Steam: Most often, water is heated by burning coal, oil, or gas. However, solar energy (from sunlight) or nuclear power can also do the job. The resulting steam turns the turbines.

3. Wind: Blowing wind spins turbines in an open field.

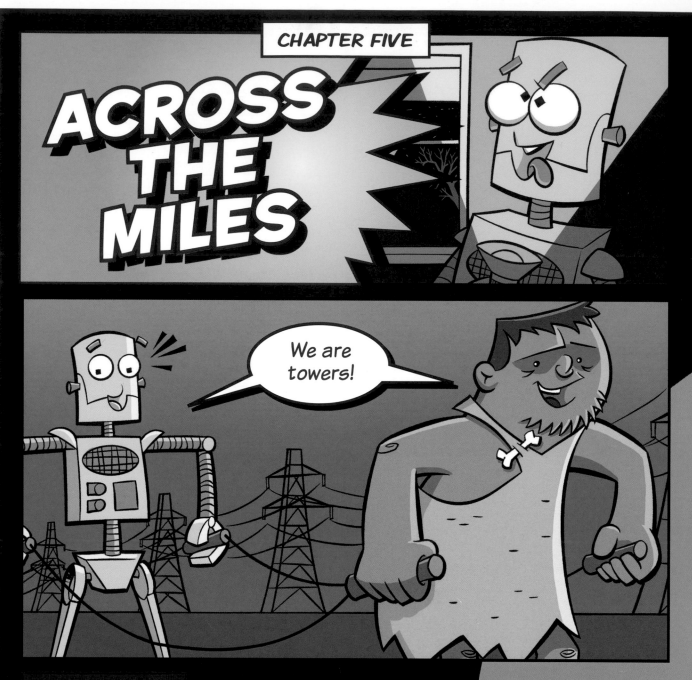

CHAPTER FIVE

ACROSS THE MILES

We are towers!

TIME LINE

600 BC
Thales, a Greek philosopher and scientist, discovers static electricity.

1600 AD
English scientist William Gilbert is the first to use the term *electricity*.

1752
Benjamin Franklin describes his kite experiment.

1800
The first electric battery is created.

Now that the electricity has been produced, how does it get to people's homes?

1. Electric current flows from the power plant to a substation. Here, electricity is fed through a **transformer**. Its job is to bump up the **voltage** to very high levels. This allows the electricity to travel long distances without losing too much energy along the way.

1821
English scientist Michael Faraday discovers the connection between electricity and magnets. His ideas are the basis for the electric motor.

1837
Thomas Davenport invents the electric motor.

1879
Thomas Edison invents the practical light bulb.

1882
Edison creates an electric power station that can power 5,000 lights.

2. This high-voltage electricity travels on thick wires on huge metal towers, often near highways.

3. The electricity reaches another substation, closer to the city. Here, a transformer lowers the voltage to a safer level.

4. This safer electricity travels along feeder lines. These lines may be buried underground. Most often, they are strung on poles. Electricity runs along the feeder lines until it reaches a small transformer right outside your house. The voltage is lowered one more time before the current enters your home.

1936
By now, electric power has been brought to most of the United States.

1974
The National Aeronautics and Space Administration (NASA) creates the first wind farm to produce electricity.

2002
The United States has increased its electricity use by more than 25 percent since 1991.

2009
Water power generates seven percent of the electricity used in the United States.

5. The wires that attach to your home are run through an electric meter. This is so the power company knows how much to charge you.

6. The wires are tied into the fuse box or circuit breaker panel in your house. The electricity flows from here to the outlets in every room.

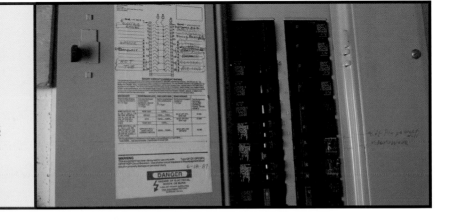

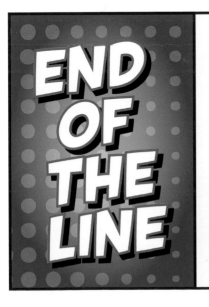

END OF THE LINE

Wait a minute, doesn't the electricity have to travel back to the power plant to make a complete circuit? Yes! It actually travels back to the power plant through the earth. Outside every house, there is a long copper rod driven into the ground. This keeps the electricity flowing from the power plant to your house and back again.

WHO TURNED OUT THE LIGHTS?

There are ten seconds left in the Super Bowl. Your team has the ball on the ten-yard line. If they score, they win the game. You lean forward in your seat. The ball is hiked, the quarterback drops back to pass. . . . Suddenly, everything goes black.

It's a blackout—power to your home has been interrupted. It can last a few minutes, a few hours, or even days. Blackouts are typically caused by weather. Ice building up on the power lines can cause them to snap. Strong winds can pull wires off the house.

CHAPTER SIX

A BETTER WAY

In the United States, nearly 70 percent of power plants rely on coal, oil, or natural gas to generate electricity. But these **fossil fuels** come with two main problems.

1. We're Running Out

These resources are getting harder and harder to find. Also, they are nonrenewable—once we use them up, they are gone.

2. Global Warming

Burning fossil fuels gives off harmful greenhouse gases. These gases trap heat inside Earth's atmosphere the way the windows trap heat inside your car on a sunny day.

That causes **global warming**. Higher temperatures can lead to all kinds of strange and scary stuff, like more droughts, floods, and hurricanes.

Give Me Clean Energy!

Wind, water, and solar power can all be used to create electricity. They are three forms of clean, renewable energy. They don't cause global warming, and they will never run out.

In 2009, renewable energy sources generated only 10 percent of electricity in the United States. What's the holdup?

1. Weather

These resources depend on the weather. To spin a wind turbine, you need a windy day. A solar panel needs a sunny day. Batteries or back-up resources are needed.

2. Money

Electricity from water is as cheap or cheaper as electricity generated by fossil fuels, but the same is not true for wind and solar power. Sure, wind and sunlight are free. But the required technology is not free. Wind energy can cost twice as much as energy from fossil fuels, and solar energy is three to six times the price. As technology improves, though, these prices will come down.

3. Location

The windiest places may not be where most people live. Power plants that depend on water have to be on a river or other water source. More power lines may be needed to bring the electricity to where it's needed.

4. Wildlife

Power plants that rely on water power change the flow of rivers and lakes. This can harm the wildlife that lives there. Flying animals such as birds and bats are sometimes killed when they accidentally fly into the blades of wind turbines.

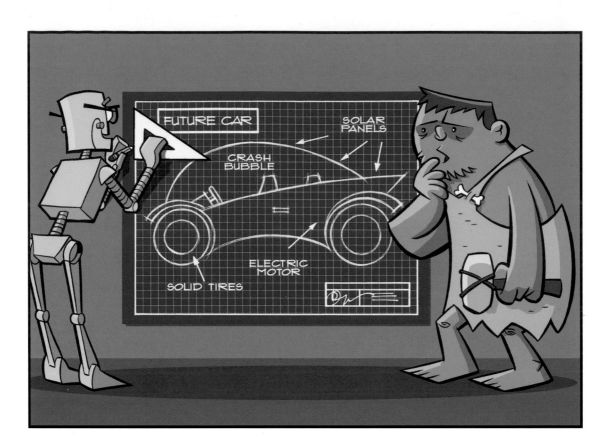

Looking Ahead

Electricity use in the United States is going up every year. As more new and exciting electronic gadgets become available, our demand will only rise.

The future of the planet depends on renewable energy—making it more available, more efficient, and cheaper. Scientists and lawmakers are working hard to make it happen. With some great ideas and a lot of help (maybe from you!), we might just get there.

WAYS TO SAVE

Chances are, the electricity in your home and school comes from fossil fuels. Someday that will change. Until then, what can you do to save energy? Here are a few simple ideas:

1. Turn off lights when you don't need them.
2. Power down your computer when you aren't using it.
3. Make sure your washing machine is full every time you use it.
4. Use less water when taking a shower. After all, energy was used to heat it up.
5. Use the battery on your MP3 player or cell phone until it is completely out instead of recharging all the time. This will make the battery more efficient.
6. Play real sports instead of video-game sports.

HOW WE SAVED
ENERGY TODAY
- hung clothes on clothesline
- played outside
- unplugged Robot when he took a nap

WORDS TO KNOW

conductors (kun-DUK-tuhrs): Conductors are substances that electricity can flow through. Conductors are usually metal.

electric circuit (ih-LEK-trik SUR-kit): An electric circuit is the path that electricity must flow on in order to be useful. An electric circuit makes a complete loop and only works if it is not broken.

electrons (ih-LEK-trons): Electrons are parts of atoms that orbit around the centers. Electricity is the flow of electrons from one place to another.

fossil fuels (FOS-uhl FYOOLZ): Fossil fuels include oil, coal, and natural gas. Most power plants burn fossil fuels to generate electricity.

generator (JEN-uh-ray-tuhr): A generator is the part of a power plant where electricity is generated. Inside a generator, electricity is made by magnets spinning inside coils of copper wire.

global warming (GLOH-buhl WAWRM-ing): Global warming is the increase in Earth's average temperature. Burning fossil fuels causes global warming.

transformer (trans-FOR-muhr): A transformer is a device that changes the voltage of electricity. It steps up voltage to allow electricity to travel more easily along a power line or lowers voltage to make electricity safe for home use.

voltage (VOHL-tihj): Voltage is the ability to push electric current. Voltage is increased and decreased by transformers as electricity flows from a power plant to a house.

FIND OUT MORE

Visit our Web site for links about how electricity works: childsworld.com/links

Note to Parents, Teachers, and Librarians: We routinely verify our Web links to make sure they are safe and active sites. So encourage your readers to check them out!

INDEX